Those Days

Olivia Ell

Presentation by *BookLeaf Publishing*

Web: www.bookleafpub.com

E-mail: info@bookleafpub.com

ISBN: 9789357696333

First edition 2022

DEDICATION

This is dedicated to my family for always trying to lift my spirits. and especially thank you to my 7th grade English teacher for exposing me to my love of writing (Ms. Guidry)

PREFACE

I have suffered depression from my early teen years unsure of why I felt that way I did. Knowing that my life could have been worse and isn't actually that bad only seemed to worsen the illness. When I graduated high school I didn't know how to cope in an adult world. Now 22 and although I'm still struggling, I started doing something different. I started to write down the things that made me happy, I wrote down my thoughts; and I wrote my troubles all in the forms of poems, lists, and narratives. This is a collection of how I process my emotions and how I understand that some of those days aren't my whole life.

These Days

Let's not forget
The time when storms flowed over.
Let's not forget,
How the thundering skies
Electrified the sky.
Let's not forget those days
Let's not forget

But let's not linger either…
Let's not forget happy days
Let's not forget calm days
Some days may be ugly
But not all days
Let's not forget those days

Take a Little Time

Busy, busy, world
Buzzing all around our ears
Never sounding right,
Always starting fights.

Dizzy, dizzy, world
All too much to see
Always blinding lights
Never experiencing the sights

Smelly, smelly, world
Enticing such sickening scents
Never smelling that delicious bite
Always nauseating

Touchy, touchy, world
Giving too much sensation
Always overwhelming
Never feeling right

Stop, world, stop
Take a little time
Time to listen,
Time to experience,
Time to taste,
Time to feel

Stop, world, stop
Take a little time
Time to rest,
Time to breathe,
Ready one, two, three

It's not as easy as it seems
Not as easy to remember
Everything moves so quickly
Nothing seems to simmer

Stop. World. Stop
Just take a little time
Take your time
To understand your life

Aware

When I look in the mirror
All I see is me.
Simple as that.
Yet in a way I don't feel free

A pick here and a pick there
Always a pick on me
I'll never see
What beauty lies beneath

I want to though…
I want to see…
Me…
I am she…

No matter how I'll be
I always try to see
Me…
My beauty is the key

Some days are hard
When I am blind
And all i can think
Is ugly

Those days are not my best
Those thoughts are not
Me…
I just want to be free

Besides those days
That's when i can see
My curly hair, wild and lively
My freckles, sunkissed and tiny
My smiles, sweet and kindly
My hands, delicate and handy
My legs alive and spritely
My… Beauty?

When I look in the mirror
All I see is me
How beautiful I am
I am free.

In These Fields

6

The song of the whispers in these weeds flow gently
across the breeze to say 'I love you'
The soil beneath my feet roots me and my memories
How lovely the dandelions console me drifting
wishes kiss my eyes and promes me...
'you are lovely'

A Coven Meets

Every Tuesday night we play to the sound of our
laughter.
Cards, boards, pieces and dice all scatter the floor,
each one filled with memories.
The scrunched faces, the tears, and the honest truths
seeped through our teeth.
our chants echoes through the night, as it sings a soft
lullaby to the moon.
The mayhem and the hijinks of the witches in our
family cast spells at our leisure.
Three generations of witches...
or brujas as they say...
all gather every Tuesday.

Lemons

8

Someone once told me that life was like lemons.
Sour, bitter, and nasty all by itself
When you taste them you clench your fist at the
heavens
but add a little sugar and water then those troubles
just melt.

If you add salt your taste buds retract.
that salt is nothing but more bad.
If you just had sugar your life just lacked.
That sugar is all the good firsthand.

Your life is water waiting to be flavored
with Sugar and lemons completes the bittersweet
savor .

Silent

9

What lovely memories sing to us
sung by Warblers dreaming to be free.
Nightmares pulling and causing our distrust,
daydreams guiding and playing with glee.

How nice to remember it so pleasant
I can only wish to thrive in hopes
But I never seem to remember it
happy times that are stuck in my throat.

I wish to live free from anxiety
but here I am stuck quietly.

Wild

Wild women grow like wallflowers in the snow
It's nothing like how they expect it to be
Bursting from the cold they dance and give us a show
Singing and playing knowing they're free.

Let's redefine our femininity
The values of ourselves that hold us high
Let's explore the history of our divinity
When man had whispered a strong lie

Wild women is what we are
So why not raise the bar.

Overwhelming pressure

Ever felt so tense?
Beaten?
Worn?
All at your expense?

I hate that.
I hate the praise we earn to overexert.
I hate the rewards to out burn
I hate that.

If for only one day I could stop time
I would do all the things to call my body mine.

What would I do you ask?
I would stop and simply take a breath
Tell myself to slow down
You won't live for long
So take your time to enjoy your life
Because respect is your first round.

Crows

I often find humans to be much like crows
As social as they are,
They are never alone.
One crow, two crows, more crows, no crows.
With family coming first,
It's no wonder why they talk
Collecting little trinkets
Holding each memory
Never seeming to have a mind fog.
Humans are a lot like crows
Chirping happily and flapping their wings.
They will never be alone.

Picture Perfect

Take pictures of everything
From your smile to your skies
Because nothing will ever beat the moment in
that time

The feeling of joy and laughter from pictures of
your friends
The feeling of sorrow of missing the old times

Most importantly take photos of you,
Even if it's just your hands, you legs, or the
freckles on your cheeks
Let yourself remember
Let your strength speak.

I am alive

It's tiring to smile
So give it a rest
Shut your eyes
It might be awhile.

It's okay to stop and take moments
We don't have many to take
So breathe
It soon becomes a vital component.

Take your time and see
Remind yourself you are not selfish
Your life is yours
So enjoy it.

I used to stand outside
Feel the wind on my skin
Remind myself that this...
This is what it means to be alive

To breathe
To see
To feel
That is what it means

What is True Worth

15

It may take a while
To find someone other than you
And to love every part

Keep in mind that you are worthy
Worthy of loving eyes
Those soft touches
Someone to call you mine

You are worthy of warm embraces,
Lovely affirmations

You are worthy of love
Don't ever forget that

Little things

Play with the toys
The ones you never got

Read all the books
You never had time for

Enjoy all the food
You have been wanting to try

Burn the candles
You have been saving for a good time

Wear that cute dress
You saved for a good date

Put on your favorite face mask
You wear when you want to relax

Don't stop yourself
From enjoying what makes you happy

Grow

Feel the roots beneath your feet
Let them grow
Let them be

Crawling up your spine
Oh what it is to be alive

Feel the leaves sprout from your branches
Let them cover
Let them discover

Inching towards the sun
Your growth has begun

Feel the flowers that you spring
Let them bloom
Don't assume

Growing from your being
You are you
And that is just beautiful

You will grow until you can't anymore
And when you think you are done
A surprise will then come

Life is full of experience
You'll never stop seeing
So continue to grow
Until there's nothing left anymore.

Haiku for death

Death isn't goodbye
Death is loving what is gone
Love will never die

Goodbye

Before I go
I wish to tell you
Goodbyes aren't easy
But loving you always was

I still think about those times
How it could've changed
But all that matters is...
My heart is unwavering

Could I have done better to show you that I love you
Or could I have done better to keep you my friend
A lot of what if's stir in my mind
Because when it comes to you
Was I really kind?

I have to forgive the past
I have to keep moving on
Why is it so hard
That those feelings last?

I forgive you
Not you as in you
But you as in me
I forgive you

You couldn't have known
Things would turn out like this
So it's better to understand
And forgive as it is hard to resist.

I forgive you
Not you as in you
But you as in me
I forgive you

Now rest because you'll forgive too.

Those days

Let's not forget those days
Let's not forget

But let's not linger either…
Let's not forget happy days
Let's not forget calm days
Some days may be ugly
But not all days
Let's not forget those days

I try to remember those days
Those days when I feel like me
It's better than other days
And overall I only wish to continue healing.

Let's not forget those days.

www.ingramcontent.com/pod-product-compliance
Lightning Source LLC
LaVergne TN
LVHW021354200726
843509LV00014B/2843